THE DAMAGES

THE DAMAGES

Poems by

RICHARD HOWARD

Wesleyan University Press

MIDDLETOWN, CONNECTICUT

Acknowledgement is gratefully made to the following magazines, in whose pages some of these poems have appeared: *Circle Review, Craft Horizons, For Now, Quarterly Review of Literature,* and *Tri-Quarterly.*

"Bonnard: A Novel," "A Far Cry After a Close Call," and "Private Drive" part ii (there titled "The Landscape Garden") were first printed in *The New Yorker.*

"Crepuscular," "The Difference," "Secular Games," and "209 Canal" were originally published in *Poetry.*

Library of Congress Catalog Card Number: 67–24112
Manufactured in the United States of America
First edition

To Sanford Friedman

The mind certain of its meat
The heart's law undisputed

CONTENTS

I

II

III

THE DAMAGES

I

A FAR CRY AFTER A CLOSE CALL

> For if they do these things in a green tree what
> shall be done in the dry?
>   —*Luke* 23:31.

Nuns, his nieces, bring the priest in the next
Bed pralines, not prayers for the next world,
        But I've had one look myself
        At *that* one (looking

Back now, crammed in the convalescent ward,
With the invisible man opposite
        Sloshing most of the Black Sea
        Around in his lungs,

While the third patient coughs and borrows *Time*).
No one turned over when I was wheeled in;
        The efficient British nurse
        Snipped off my soggy

Trousers and put me right, "sure as Bob's your
Uncle." The water roared and ran away,
        Leaving only words to stock
        My mind like capsules

Crowding a bottle. Then the lights blew up,
Went out, someone was going through My Things
        While I rowed—rowed for my life
        Down the rubber floor—

But the waves failed me. The hallway heaved where I
Foundered and turned in my doctor's dry hands
      To sovereign selflessness:
          Meaning had melted.

"Mon corps est moi," Molière said. They're more than that,
This monster the body, this miracle
      Its pain—when was I ever
          Them, when were they me?

At thirty-three, what else is there to do
But wait for yet another great white moth
      With eager, enlarging eyes
          To land on my chest,

Slowly, innocently choking me off?
The feelers stir while I lie still, lie here
      (Where on earth does it come from,
          That wind, that wounding

Breath?), remembering the future now,
Foreseeing a past I shall never know,
      Until the little crisis
          Breaks, and I wake.

For as Saint Paul sought deliverance from
The body of this death, I seek to stay—
      Man is mad as the body
          Is sick, by nature.

SEFERIADES: A Poem in Two Parts

For Michael Lekakis

i

How much like life itself, to know
    his midwest translator, not
the Middle-Eastern troglodyte
    shambling onto the platform
led by my suave scholarly friend.
    Later, when his own turn came,
I was to learn if not the source
    of what had doused me, at least
then the delta it headed for,
    a plausible jet of all
that heroic jabber. Now we were
    just marking time until it
ran by us, not even words but
    a welter of speech dissolved
in a watery idiom.
    Afterwards would come the words,
the tragic cosmopolitan
    lies, lessons from an exile,
Smyrna oranges and laments.
    The famous foreign poet
mounted the stream of utterance:
    his palms, an oily capital,
propped that marble head, enormous,
    stained brown like ruins, rocking
mournfully on his round shoulders,
    measuring the monologue
of an old man's voice that dribbled
    out of an old woman's mouth.

Twitching in the chair beside me,
    the Greek I had invited
for comfort, a cushion against
    my Barbarian's conscience,
whispered to himself, while Something
    spoken on the stage extracted
from his hands, that lay like mallets
    in his lap, the convulsive
gestures of protest or pleasure—
    I could not tell, but only
that habits had been changed, hidden
    or laid bare, and still the Voice
which was a waste to me, to him
    ecstasy caught in its act,
ran on, the Poem persisting
    whenever its syllables
threatened to dissolve in the sands
    of a cadence completed.
Abruptly, in that guttural
    wilderness (not one meaning
but a movement among meanings
    possible), I recognized—
desperate, no doubt, for a hold
    on any knowledge—the word
for "river," then the word for "sun."
    And as in life, when the words
come, the meanings waken: "River . . .
    Sun." I waited for the rest.

Obscure behind the lectern where
    the laureate subsided
but would not be still, inveighing
    against silence as against
"Izmir," the willing translator

waited, licked his lips, ready
though the alien voice prevailed,
    the bald dome careening, eyes
down and darkened, into discourse.
    Peering at my friend, whose part
was yet to come, where he hovered
    like a cape of qualms behind
that Mediterranean headland,
    I waited too, suddenly
discovering I knew the word
    for "man" and the word for "life"
and the word for "river" again.
    Then, many times, the word for
"god" came, and just as suddenly
    it was over, the old Greek
clawing at the mike they had draped
    around his neck on a dead
garland, and even our applause
    could not drown out his choking;
my friend the bearded professor
    offered to help, but the Master
fought him off, won free, and waved him
    to the stand he stumbled from.

Now it was not so much like life,
    but I could make out the words,
all of them, in a long lament
    about Helen, false Helen
who was not at Troy—a linen
    undulation there, a thing
of air—while Mrs. Menelaus
    languished, for real, on the Nile
—not Ilion but her nails ruined
    by a brown river, the sun

baking an empty land, "on the lip
    of Egypt," and Paris lay
with nothing more than a shadow,
    and the others were slaughtered
for nothing, for a Helen's sake.
    Then came the place where the word
for "god" had been lisped so often:
    "O nightingale, nightingale,"
my friend read out cold, careful not
    to try for a rhapsode's tone,
the typed sheet trembling a little
    in his hands: "O nightingale!
(three times, *aïdóni*, to the ear
    anonymous) What is a god?
What is not a god? What is the life
    in between god and not-god?"
Unwreathed beside him, the old man
    nodded: that was how it went;

that was the claim he recognized,
    a clamor in the mind, so
he knew what came next, the end came:
    "And messengers were sent off
to tell him, when their lungs allowed,
    how much suffering, so much
of life had fallen from the light,
    so much into the abyss,
and all for a shifting garment,
    for no more than a Helen."
Again the applause, but this time
    as if our hands understood
what to our ears before had been
    the wrong tide of sound turning.
The diffident reader deferred,

abashed, to clapping that washed
over the old head like a stream
    caressing a brown boulder
in its boisterous course. Beside me
    the Greek was up, murmuring
something about a myth, and rushed
    back to embrace the poet,
both of them crying, and in all
    that crowd of gratulating
Hellenes bearing gifts, what better
    could I do than ask my Greek
to come and meet my friend, his friend's
    American translator?

ii

Across the little lake, a mile
    from where we were standing, stark
against the fingernail of sand
    that scarred our summer's blue frieze,
we could still see her, a moving
    figure, tiny now and black
at this distance as she was blond
    close up, close to the color
of her tremulous beach, the mild
    sublime that in the Maine air
beckoned still, opposite our dock.
    Six of us, tired blue-lipped boys,
traded rabbit punches between
    goose pimples, staring hard
over the water all that while
    we were waiting for our coach
to tell us the time we had made,
    impatient though for more

than our trophies, peering
         across the twice-lapped lake, less
a medium now than a mood,
         at the mysterious dame
who had met us there and offered
         jasmine tea, toadstools that came
apart before we could take them
         from her long white hands—but then
suddenly she had sent us home
         like boys. Or did we escape?

In any case, we got away,
         happy now we had taken
the chance, the test, the rehearsal
         of ourselves thrusting us on:
swimming the mile over, the mile
         back, one odd hour's rest between—
one hour at best outside the shack
         of the weirdo in the woods.
She fed us, humming to herself,
         touching Jimmy where his suit
sagged, playing with him just like that:
         "What is all this juice and all
this joy?" And who knew what to say?
         Now, after the lake, the planks
burned, and where their shadows landed
         on its pea-green surface, boulders
showed between the slats: we could see
         fish in their slow enterprise,
as if the water really was
         a weaker form of ice. The sun
drew circles on the lake, their rim
         being that scalp of white sand
before which her shawls hung upon

the wind, imitating still
the gestures of our crawl, the way
    a man puts on the shadow
he walks into. She had spoken . . .
    to all of us? to Jimmy? me?

"The cup," she said, "drink this, it will
    make you immortal — take it."
Remembering, we laughed at her,
    a mile away and only
a nature-creep now, some kind of
    fae in the forest. Eager
for our counsellor to inspect,
    we shouldered each other to
the brink, searching for places where
    immortality would show
first. Little waves smacked at the dock:
    underneath the boards the wood
was slimy, rotting, cold. Jimmy
    shivered, and just then our coach
appeared, working down the hillside
    to the dock, whistle bobbing
on the lanyard around his neck,
    the sun by now powerless
against his brown bald head. Never
    hurrying, he just happened
to be wherever it was hoped,
    and when: a man left over
from an age when the old men lived
    and the young men died. I told
him what had happened, or I told
    what the six of us thought
had happened: they were not the same
    stories, but he heard them out.

"Each of you drank," he said. "Now which . . ."
        and set to work, confident
we would not betray our chances
        of divinity, for all
the ridicule we had mustered.
        Wisest of men, he devised
a graver stratagem: at once
        his hands, withered by water
more than by the years, sounded out
        our bodies, easy over
the clammy limbs, expert, depraved,
        relentless, palpating where
the portal skin lay slack, prying
        at the reluctant muscles,
smoothing flesh where it would pucker
        and the hair, already rough
in hollows where it soon would curl.
        "She said it would make us gods
if we didn't tell!" Donald shrieked,
        and the old man nodded, hands
languid, sure. He had been across
        the lake, our sullen weedy
watering place; had visited
        as others were probably
visiting now—why else had she
        dismissed us?—a witches' world,
the site we have all, at one time,
        discovered, created, lost.

For this he was our waterfront
        familiar, rummaging now
among our bones sleeved in their still
        uncertain flesh distempered
by scratches, bites, sliding over

scars already blurred by tan,
an old man talking to himself,
　　　as one grudging the future
to what is of no use to him,
　　　until he straightened and spoke
to the six, naked before him,
　　　cuffing the last boy in line:
"Silly as you are, stunned by what
　　　she has done or made you do,
bruised by a lurching behavior
　　　like the lake's, sore from the loss
of what you left behind, you pocked
　　　peeling children, even so"—
and the solemn words met and moved
　　　in our minds like speaking lips—
"not one boy among you could I
　　　dare to single out and say,
'You, my friend, you are not a god.'"
　　　Across the water, the beach
winced now and wrinkled in the glare:
　　　she was going away and
we could see her going; once gone,
　　　the sun's white circle widened.

Levin, on his way to Kitty's love,
Saw children walking in a row to school,
Bluish doves flying down from the eaves
And little floury loaves thrust out
By an unseen hand. "It all happened at once,"
Tolstoy says: a boy ran suddenly
Toward a dove and glanced back, smiling,
At Levin. The dove flew up, wheeling,
And the snowflakes glittered in the sun.
From the windows came a smell of fresh bread
And the loaves were put out. Remember?
So much grace Tolstoy grants without God.

"It all happened at once," once at midnight
In that unseasonable fall of ours—
It seemed to me the universe slowed down
And lingered in a climate of its choice
As if without the Law. I had a sense
Of something ceded, something given over
In that bad autumn, when day after day
The city warmed, its summer smells restored
To a tempting lie. All our sparrows stayed
While even migratory birds confined
Their circulation, did not go, but hung
Upon the hindered weather like a curse.

I reached our crooked corner where the night
Unwinds. Like Levin, I was on my way.
Slowly the citizens moved past, so many
Allegories of choice, most of them gay
As bright October's wreck or brazenly
Concealing the winter to come. Over us loomed
The ladies' prison where The Girls called down
Inaccurate obscenities to us

Or to each other, inside out. Above
Our 'rescued' Ruskin courthouse roof
The tower held its numb Gothic dial
Gold as a medal against the dim sky.

There I stood among The Boys, marvelling
While they murmured by me like a stream
Beneath the shouting girls, shorn Rapunzels
In their castle keep, and stared above
At the clock, at the unfeeling sky
Above even that, wondering what wind
Bearded with snowflakes like Tolstoy's God
Could carry off our grief, could save us
Or by leaving soothe? Was liberty
To leave enough? It was enough to stay,
To inhabit earth, where we do not stay
But unlike God in heaven, come and go.

First I had a dream of water,
    then one of rotting.
Your eyes, loosened from their arches,
    were salt ponds, sinking,
and your lips opened like a sluice:
    I failed to follow
the juice where it ran down, rinsing
    a deeper hollow.

The decaying dream worked upward—
    this time I could not
bear to see a jelly taking
    your face, fast, away.
But waking, I extol waking,
    for I cannot call
you to mind without energy:
    movements of making.

I have the will to win over
    rot and water both,
to recover dreams by turning
    them true, thus earning
back what I spent by night. Coming
    is a coming to,
learning by the body's wet spoil
    to endure morning.

SEEING COUSIN PHYLLIS OFF

The SS France, *Second Class, Cabin* U–20

Few sights were lovelier
Than my watch laved in the *brut* champagne
Exploding from a jiggled magnum.
Your foreign cabin-mates' *schadenfreude*
        Helped them help each other
        To more caviar, and your handsome
        Husband brushed me off, as handsome does;
Wizened by a decade of adultery,
        You whispered some final
        Instructions under the din, patted
        Your graying bun: for a dozen years
The sacred fount had been flowing in his
        Favor, and you knew it.
        In Paris, a daughter was pregnant,
        Unmarried, impatient for your next
Round of meddling to begin. The cycle
        Of all our messy lives
        Alters so little from war to war
        I wonder how any of us
Dares to hope for a private happiness.
        Wilde said what we want is
        Pleasure, not happiness—it has more
        Tragic possibilities. Your caviar
Must be second-class too: I miss the old
        Normandie, Narrenschiff
        Of our fashionable thirties. Now
        The diesels suddenly start to throb
In a sickening vibrato that drives
        The implacable screw
        Up through even the *pont supérieur.*

My stomach turns, but all the champagne
Is gone, except for the foam in my watch,
            I nod at the nightmare
            Of a class that we both belong to:
Repetition, and hurry away
To give your worried lover messages.
                  My poor mad Cousin Phyl,
            No use trying to drown time on these
            Harridan voyages of ours — once
They called them maiden — not by wet watches
            Or even dry champagne.

TO AEGIDIUS CANTOR

*Inculpated for heresy before the Episcopal
Court at Cambrai, 1411*

Only you would find it easy to believe
    What we are about these days
Or at least these nights, for little that we do
    Is likely to amaze you,
Minister who flung open the doors of your
    Adamite conventicle
And having suffered the high inspiration
    Of the Holy Ghost (the which
Visited you as you lay with the Brethren
    In quivering chastity),
Ran out into the street, "a long way stark
    Naked," wearing on your head
A platter of meat. It must have been a dark
    Village whose urbanity
You ruffled, while our town of course is klieg-lit
    Wherever there might be cause
For danger. Yet if we didn't go you one
    Better, then we went as far
Lately, arranging to have our chargers full
    Of fish, flesh and fowl, bloody
Sausages and all, dump in a lumpy stream
    Upon the bodies of six
Bikini-bare girls and boys disporting there
    On stage—the lineaments
Of galvanized desire—painting each other
    Pleonastically red,
And we labelled it "Meat Joy." A Happening.

It is because events, for us, are sacred
      In themselves, without the need
For any concentrated sign, any Writ,
      That I wanted to write you
(To whom our dim question: "Yes, but is it art?"
      Would never have occurred);
To us, you see, it is what occurs that counts,
      That becomes art —we call *art*
Holy these days, which is why we are concerned
      With what it is. No longer
Just theater, though the catharsis was there,
      More than fun, it was a physick
You set out to serve, patching the sick pavements
      Of Cambrai with blood. The power
Of your nakedness, metaphor of the meat
      You wore as a kind of crown,
The charismatic carnal emanations
      Not only from the salver
But from yourself—white skin, black hair, the limbs
      We see in Bosch and Cranach—
Such things could heal. And it is healing we seek,
      An art that will medicine
To selfhood and malnutrition of impulse.
      We covet your conception,
After our comical ways, for there is one
      Knowledge shared: we know the health
Of the City cannot be secret. Raw meat
      Serves, when served up in the raw,
To remind us of the life running under
      The hairy skin, red that must
Keep us comfortable by being kept inside.
      Few deign to show, or dare to,
Where it keeps, and yet the blood is there, helping
      Matters happen all the time;

Small wonder we revere the occurrences
    That spatter our streets with gore—
Mere events, call them, performances, ventures
    Which having been made become
The going on of things, the enduring flow.

    Take another time, to wit
One April in Paris, Dali dropped an ox
    Flayed and dripping to the stage
As emblematic climax to a ballet
    Among the gasps and greasy
Legs of girls, the painted drops still running while
    The curtain fell, and the riot
Which followed surprised no one, of course. Silly,
    That sympathetic magic
Must have seemed to you, but inevitable
    To carnivores, and meaning,
For all our burlesque, much what you had in mind:
    Human love resists the body
It inhabits, its old enemy and friend.
    Cantor, I remember you
And prize your heretic episode the more
    Because I praise what we do:
There is a pitch past cruelty as past love
    When all flesh acquires the same
Queer smell. Then the order of our blood commands,
    Enforces a discipline
Though never a predictable one. Say
    It is the mess we live by,
Made into a joy. The meat joy. You know. Thanks.

THE LOVER SHOWETH WHEREFORE HE IS ABANDONED OF THE BELOVED HE SOMETIME ENJOYED, EVEN IN SLEEP

Tonight (the moonless kind
That Judith might have spent
In Holofernes' tent
Until her ravished victim found
His final ravishment)
The many come to mind
Who lately came and, coming, later went,

Taking a way you must
Soon take yourself, I trust,
While by the brazen laws
That league diversion with disgust
Those others plead their cause
Elsewhere, to the applause
I lavished best when they deserved it least.

I lean now on your bed
And trace a pulsing vein
That proves you are not dead:
Dividing us, that other Red
Sea dandles you within
Its tides until you deign
To wake and make the sea divide again.

Each of us peers into
Mirrors for what is true
About the rest: mostly
We spend our spare time in the blue
Movies of memory.
We are blind seeing, see
Blind, and find our way the way moles do.

Moved but unmoving, I
Sit here and stare your sleep
Out of countenance. My
Crude hopes crumble to a heap
As retrospectively
I sift what I would keep
Of all such savored, severed fellowship:

Tall in my mind stands one
(I seldom heard him speak)
Whose only lifelong work
Was burnishing the boyhood on
His face; and one whose look
I know, though I have known
No likes of him: unlikely guest, he's gone

(Our neighborly disgrace)
Without a proper name;
Here's one I had for whom
No second act, or try, or time
Was real; another whose
Fortunes went up in flame—
His ghost, among the ghosts, in ashes goes.

But let the darkness fall
Politely on them all:
The past must have an end.
Your dreaming body and my mind
Alone at last contend.
Courageously I send
My thought against you while your mute limbs loll

At enviable ease.
You lie without surprise

Beside me as I wait
For clues: the file is incomplete.
    Who is it that you meet
    When your round shoulders rise
And shed your hands like dead leaves on the sheet?

    You sigh and smile and seem
    Released. I ask you where
    You've been. What is the home
You visit while in exile here?
    As if you couldn't care
    Less (your record is clear)
You answer in a trance, "I never dream."

EUSEBIUS TO FLORESTAN: ON APROSEXIA

Prince, pity me then, for it is an ill
Uncircumstanc'd save as the air inscribes,
When if I lose the tenth of what I have
I'm lost. After comes a time when if I keep
The tenth of what I have I shall be saved;
Even as the lamb that feeds on what
Has melted in the mouth, runs down
Into the heart, and cannot name the taste.

Prince, what days are these! I stare
Into the sun with hatred, it will make
The winter worse. Mortality
And the dim senses are my reason only.
There is no dark endeavor in my love,
But lately when I look'd into your eyes
That gleam like incandescent grapes
Or listen'd to the sounds, ling'ring still,
Of your speech within my ear, echoings
I have not had since Word was made Flesh,
It was as if I sudden saw the waves
Obey when I struck the sea and said: Take me!

Happiness is an embarrassment (men say,
In truth, that the material world is but
A fiction, though any other is nightmare).
Thereto so unsuited am I that my bearing,
Prince, grows awkward if it is too great:

The peacock would be overcome by glory
Were he not accustom'd to it from the start.
Today I have search'd my solitude, Prince,
For your grace, but a man's genius is wearied
By the habit of hoping: I forget, therefore I am.

CREPUSCULAR

Late in the afternoon the light
    at this tapering end
of Long Island not so much fails
    as filters out the sun,
and in a month amid stances
    restores the word twilight
to its original senses:
    the day between, or half
itself, as when Locke alluded
    to 'the twilight of probability.'

But if at this moment I see
    its application, still
the word comes hard, appalling me
    in poetry: it sounds
too much like toilet, and Verlaine
    becomes impossible
to translate, for instance, even
    when the real thing happens
around me, as at this moment.
    Should reality sound poetical?

I sit at the French window (why
    else worry about Verlaine?)
worrying too about Robert Frost
    who said either we write
out of a strong weakness (poets
    love oxymoronic forms)
for the Muse, or we write because
    it seems like a good idea
to write. As the day tapers off
    like the island, I wonder at my choice.

Indeed, have I chosen? Outside
    the open window, Max
the dog is staring in at me,
    I can still see him, pale
against the darkening lawn, now,
    for he is a white dog
that has just found out the difference
    between Inside and Outside,
the choice that always, when there is
    a door, even a French one, must be made.

Thresholds for Max have lately meant
    a problem: he lies across
the sill supposing, I suppose,
    he'll have the best of both —
whatever world looms on each side;
    why, as another French
romantic said, must a door be
    either open or shut?
Max whines if I go to the toilet
    and close him out—for him the word toilet

clearly suggests the twilight, some
    subliminal ending.
These French doors ajar (ah, Musset!)
    merely frustrate decision;
and as the moments modify
    each blade of grass, blossom,
bush and branch, suddenly showing,
    in a light committed
to impartiality, yet
    another aspect: the night side of things,

Max trots over to the window
        where I sit wondering
if I want to elope with her
        or just be good friends, more
like a brother to the Muse, and
        gravely—I guess it is
gravely, in fact I'll never know—
        shoves his white face against
the pane, nose flattened, of the door
        and barks at me for being inside it.

But if I join him on the lawn
        that is gray now, he will
only dash back to the table
        where I have been, and bark
at me out on the silver grass.
        The Muse indoors, or on
the road? Possessed, or befriended?
        Choice is impossible.
Robert Frost is impossible.
        Max and I know the truth, quite possibly,

that the light survives a long time
        here on Long Island as
elsewhere, and then will come to terms
        with darkness, and we call
the terms *evening,* our term for time
        when neither power has
dominion, the air balances,
        but just for now, and then
the odds are on the dark again.
        Max and I know this too: it will be night.

II

INTIMATIONS OF MORTALITY

The case grows more interesting the more I get
to understand the man. He has certain qualities
very largely developed: selfishness, secrecy and
purpose. His redeeming quality is a love of ani-
mals, though, indeed, he has such curious turns
in it that I sometimes imagine he is only ab-
normally cruel.

—From Dr. Seward's diary,
in Dracula *by Bram Stoker*

i

This little boy I was
Collected other lives,
Saved them up to spoil: not gullible
Prey—goldfish in the brown lily pond
Or the old bulldog—no, he was out
　　After strange gods and not
　　Familiars. Look for him
Working his way down the privet hedge,
Clapping bees in a cyanide jar,
His grandmother's long darning needle
　　Sliding them by like beads
Until he is garlanded with a lei
Of gored furies dying on the thread.
Or find him, tomorrow, playing house
Underneath that same murmuring hedge,
　　When a fieldmouse almost
　　Runs right into his hands:
An hour's "play" is enough to make out
Of what had once been so prompt and smooth

An emblem of mouse *accidie*,
    Stupefied in his hand,
Torpid and blotchy, plainly without
Energy even to squeal or bite.
He would have to kill it: half-filled
A milk bottle, pushed the thing down in.
    It would not drown, crawling
    Up, falling back, silent,
Sad and strangely obstinate, until
He panicked, dropped the bottle, ran off
Terrified for months of some coming
    Vengeance in empty lots.

ii

    The Mouse God pursues
Me no longer, and hearing no harsh
Voices from the grass I guess the Bee
People have relented. I am free.
Today there is no more such saving up,
    Lives inevitably
    Having come to mean deaths.
I shall not be hunting any more,
But wear a string of failures, love,
Hanging stingless round my neck.
    Last night, when I returned
    From what I call real life
To you, the years lying between us
Like a hedge (the flowers fallen now),
Both of us stalled in your empty house,
The coffee as cold as the comfort,
    I saw for once, at least,
    As in a twinge of pain,
The sense of my old animal plunders:

How else do we know what we are,
Save by tokens of what we have ruined?
    How else read right the signs
Of our surrender to ourselves, save
In terms of what we are scared to save?
We mourned the time we had lost, chances
You could not keep, I could not let go.
    And I saw the future
    Impaled on its cruel coils,
A murdered mouse sliding down the glass.

i

Trying to keep out of the builders' way, we
trampled the strawberries that grew wild
and cut our fingers on red
tiles where the blood might
not show so
much.
The mud was like the Argonne trenches (pictures
we giggled over, atrocities
in the library where we
sneaked cokes and candy,
forbidden
luxe!)—
when the men went home we bled and licked our wounds
as we watched them go. There would
be something new in
this muddy field:
it was that
spring
they were building a studio with glass brick
for walls, and as we played underneath
the scaffolding you told me:
—I'm going to go
away now
so
don't be surprised to see her when she comes back.
—Who's *she,* Lois, who's coming back here?
You just smiled crooked, saying
in your grownup voice:
—Another
girl,

dressed so much like me and looking so like me
you wouldn't know it wasn't me, but
there is a way to tell, you
said, one way you'll know
I'm someone
else.
—How, Lois, how can I tell it won't be you?
—This girl, you said, will be speaking French.
—What'll I say back?—Just say
Bonjour, Mademoiselle,
and then you
ran
around the glass-brick corner (for that was when
Modern meant having corner windows)
of your father's studio,
or mother's, maybe—
it's hers now.
I
waited, sucking my thumb, incredulous but
longing for you to come back. And O
you did, but who knew how well
things would be arranged?
You *have* been
changed!
But so have I, I'm changed too, I'm you now and
everything I know of you is me:
today *I* speak French, there's been
another war, *we* do
not speak, we
spoil.

Palermo's Landscape Garden lay
South of the city
On a rock foundation—shales perforated
By intrusive gneiss, limestone caves
And lintels crannied
In soil that made an easy work of wonders:
Sudden glimpses into a Gulph,
Tunnels of baroque
Surprise from which the prospect dropt, out of sight,
To earth no more than a few feet
Below. Here we came
At springtime for annuals and in the dead
Of winter our Christmas trees
(Roots balled, re-planted
Once the tinsel, still clinging, had served its turn).
Each season, whether obelisks
Were cumbered with snow
Or yellow with the lichen-scale that lingered
In the sandstone pores, each visit,
Lois would escape
The car, our calls, and as if she had been lured
Past the terraced tubs of lemon
By the beckoning
Statuary, would dash headlong to vanish
Into the phony labyrinth
Where cypresses, black
In December, leaned together, revealing
As I ran toward the place, only
Gray mortuary
Arches, silhouetted high and hopelessly,
Which by a tweak of perspective
All at once betrayed

(Absurdly tiny) from the path that circled
    Above them, the secret old Nick
        Palermo had learned
Probably from the Greek stones in Sicily:
    Nothing has a size of its own.
        I never found her,
Lois my suburban Proserpine, summoned
    By what mystery, what message
        In those rusty rocks,
Until she was ready to appear: standing
    In pure importance at the end
        Of a corridor,
The sun braiding shadows into her bright hair,
    Or almost hidden, shivering
        Where she had waited
In a shell of dim ivy, gone to earth — gone
    For good now, as then in a game,
        With all the rigor
Fun has to have: I found you, Lois,
    Just where you left me, impatient
        To be discovered
As you had been to get away from us all
    Into a world of disciplined
        Water, distinguished
Women, even if they were only concrete
    And cracked more often than not.
        The landscape garden
You hide in now is pretty nearly the same
    As Palermo's commercial grot,
        Annuals replaced
With Everlasting Care, evergreens set out
    The way we used to do, but you
        Not — you never, you
Nowhere, now, save in that past I don't suffer

43

But create, in a ritual
              Precious to me for
Its banality. Nobody will be there
        To see you in your bush of hair
              Dance burning away,
But to me you will come, I will make you come,
        Your face saturated in sleep
              And nothing else left
In the landscape garden these late days of ours
        But darkness, Lois, and disgrace.

                        iii

        The Pierce-Arrow I took to be
              self-illustrative,
like stickpins, almost winged its way; we
        had started for the docks, at last
              the *trip* had started!
First the circuit Olmsted had laid out,
        Gothic rockeries—not Central
              but Edgewater Park,
the same system of brick tunnels, vines
        curtaining the mouths we roared
              into, hissed along,
then out into sunlight. Past the Great
        Lakes Fairground to the Flats
              where sulfur, mounded
in yellow cones like frozen custard,
        waited for the mills. *We* waited
              for the light to change:
Lois, Gramma, the chauffeur and I,
        heading downtown to the Old Pier
              where we would embark,
limousine and all, on the night boat

for the Cape. Lois sat with Gramma
        and the French bulldog
Bootsie, I was beside the chauffeur
        as the ponderous car crept up
            the gangway. "You can
drive right on!" I marvelled, Lois knew
        that all along, or said she did,
            Bootsie barked a lot
when we got to our cabin, and Fred,
        the chauffeur, disappeared into
            part of the ferry
that was fit for chauffeurs. Shuddering
        already, the black ship slid off
            after a sharp blast,
and we were away! The light had changed.

        The smell of apple peels, all
            in one scarlet worm
my Gramma could slice off not looking,
        filled the cabin where we lay
            in bed together,
"No harm," she told your mother, "at nine:
        they're only children still." Still,
            waiting for the light
to be put out in the apple-sweet air,
        I knew what I would do, what
            you were with me for
in that upper berth. Once her snoring
        started, part of the steamer
            machinery now,
I unbuttoned to your bones and rib
        by rib explored your body
            captive in my arms.
Gramma found us, saw no harm in what

she saw by the morning light:
       two children tangled
in each other's hair, mostly naked
       but only nine, and the boat
              was nearly anchored.
Fred was there, ready with the car, and
       Bootsie was more than ready.
              There was still a day's
drive, and Gramma wanted to arrive
       before the light turned, the sea
              went dark on the rocks.
Lois and Gramma shared a birthday:
       that was the treat—this whole trip
              would be a birthday
present, imagine! Gramma explained,
       giving someone the seashore
              just for being born.

Gramma this year would be a hundred
       and in my child's eye always
              was. Lois took space
on a black ship to hell, and I lost
       them both. Gramma taught me how
              to peel an apple,
how to remember, how to reach back.
       Lois wanted only to get
              safe ashore, to get
out of the stream of our animal
       perpetuations. If only
              I can keep in one
cabin the smell of apples and some
       part of that hunger to know:
              then let the light turn
bad, I will be *both* in the darkness

they left me, I won't take sides . . .
             The sea was brilliant
on the rocks my Gramma called Squeakers,
       and there seemed to be plenty
             of time. Lois must
have forgotten about the night boat,
       I decided, nothing was wrong
             anyway—I knew
more, that was all the difference it made.
       We went down to the beach where
             the tide had left signs
for Bootsie, not even unpacking
       first: Lois and I undressed
             in front of Gramma
and Fred, then the tide pools took us.
       Thrashing back, wrong to the light,
             Lois surged against me
and exclaimed as the shadows ran down
       to the water's edge, "Look, look,
             how it keeps changing!"

                    TEAR-SHEETS

       *

There was a cave under the piano
Where we could live, the animals left us
Alone there, and in the dark place behind
The pedal harp you told me you had learned
How we could have children too, whole litters
Of them if we liked! I would have to pull
Down my corduroy knickers and you would hike
Up your dress, and when our cold buttocks touched
Then they would come, the children. They have gone.

                        47

**

You hooked your legs over the crooked branch,
Your face on a level with mine, smiling,
Reversed, into my eyes as you hung there
And took great bites around your apple,
I can still hear the sound of your small teeth
Breaking the skin. There were apples all
Over the tree, and on the ground under
You as you swayed from your knobby knees. "Look!"
You cried, "I'm swallowing *up!*" Swallowed up.

***

At our progressive musicale, we danced
The Planets, I was Uranus of course
And you were one of my moons. Revolving
Until we were dizzy in our orbits
We stumbled across the gymnasium,
And our fond audience applauded us.
Across the black sky the great Figures go,
Each with its set of moons regularly
Appearing and occulted. One went out.

****

You led me into the dark kitchen where
The Monitor-top ticked and warned. Nighttime
Made the shelves creak, and the enamel chairs
Arched their backs like companionable ghosts
Of cats. I was thirsty. Gradually
In the dark, a glass was made to exist
By the white milk you poured into it. All
I could see of the invisible form
Was the ascending level. Spilled milk now.

iv

I hid behind the dying clubhouse oak
    Until my mother signalled,
Then I ran down. Lois, our big houses
Loomed above the bunkers, your new glass brick
    Blinking like a semaphor;
Mother drove, I watched the ball go by me
And the fairway led right into the trap.
    "For catching little boys?"
I asked her: was that why I was not allowed?
Words alarmed me: *course* sounded bland enough
    If ambiguous, but *links*
Meant only chains, and even the red flags
Could not make up for *traps* and *holes*
    And worst of them all, *the rough.*
I kept my distance from the olive-skinned
Sicilian caddies, so little older
    Than I was then, but living
Already in an enclave of intent
I had not ventured into yet. But when
    I did, they would still be there.

Minnows made the creeks murmur, a black dog
    I was forbidden to pet
Ran out behind me and despoiled the ninth.
But here the fauna mostly seemed to fail
    Just where it might flourish best
In this slip-cover geology: what
Bright and heraldic beasts inhabited
    These baby Himalayas,
Giant lawns, what creatures haunted these groves
Of German-silver birch? The *genius*
    Loci seemed to be a harrow,

49

And a constant drone of machines drowned out
The birds. It was a backward country, Lo,
     That beckoned to your gamey
And not quite inconsolable nights. All
At once the stories spread, a greenskeeper
     On his rounds had found you out
There with Mario, furious to see
The grounds were used for hunting after all.

     Somehow we had failed you, whom
My golfing mother called your "natural
Acquaintances," and from the guardians
     Of our games, pool boys, caddies,
Even the leathery tennis pro, you learned
A lesson that lay in wait for you, Lo,
     Waiting on the tee for lays:
What we do blurs over what we did before.
If landscape is moralized, then the course
     Addresses us both, myself
Forbidden, you a later trespasser.
I see what is linked together now, and
     What is lost. Was it the same
Thing that kept me lurking behind the oak,
Lois, while you larked out on the cold grass?
     We were the honest sportsmen
Obeying different rules for the same game,
Only I am playing still—you ended
     Black-faced on the garage floor,
The car motor running like a mower.

FURTHER INSTRUCTIONS TO THE ARCHITECT

Now about the attic: please allow
    For easy access to the roof
So Cousin Agnes can get out there.
    Fall, did you say? Remember all
The servants' bedrooms must include
A dream book in the dresser, and there was
    Always a gate across the stairs:
Our pantry sibyl walked in her sleep,
    Read tea leaves, knew what "horses" meant.

    Make sure the smell of apple peel
    Lingers in the master bedroom,
Keep lewd prints for the *Decameron*
Locked in the library, and repair
    The stained glass over the landing:
If the Lorelei's hair is still clear
The amber can always be replaced.
    I hear one ilex has fallen
Across the pond. Better plant rushes
    So the frogs will come back, evenings,
And sing their songs; restore the *allée*
Of Lombardy poplars where the doves
    Nested: we need all our mourners.

    See that the four black junipers
Don't overgrow the lawn: after dark
    The silver grass is luminous
Around them. There should be a wheezing
French bulldog on my grandmother's lap,
    Of course, and the sound of grape seeds
    Being flicked onto the porch floor
Where Ernestine is reading. Even

The corridor back to whatever
     Surprise you have in store must be
Merely the one between the (witch's)
     Kitchen and the dim hall closet
Where velveteen hangers may have turned
By now to something else unlikely.

You can't help getting it right if you
     Listen to me. Recognition
Is not to be suppressed. Why the whole
Place seems just the way it was, I tell you
     I was there last night: in dreams
We are always under house arrest.

III

BONNARD: A Novel

The tea party at Le Cannet. Just as we arrived it began,
        a downpour, and kept on.
        This might have been the time
before: Charles-Xavier playing Scriabin etudes, all the others
        at the open window.
        A landscape—lawn, garden,
strawberry patch, Japanese footbridge, barges moving on the river
        beyond—as in Verlaine
        behind a mist of rain,
and the regular noise of the rain on tens of thousands of leaves:
        such is the prose that wears
        the poem's guise at last.
White cats, one in almost every chair, pretend not to be watching
        young Jean worry the dog.
        Sophie, damp, dashes in
dishevelled from the forest, dumping out a great bag of morels
        on the table: the white
        cloth will surely be spoiled,
but the mushrooms look iridescent, like newly opened oysters
        in the raindark air, blue
        by this light. Calling it
accidental is only declaring that it exists. Then tea
        downstairs, Jean opening
        the round pantry window:
the smell of wet soil and strawberries with our cinnamon toast: all
        perception is a kind
        of sorting out, one green
from another, parting leaf from leaf, but in the afternoon rain
        signs and shadows only,

the separate life renounced,
until that resignation comes, in which all selfhood surrenders . . .
Upstairs, more Scriabin
and the perfect gestures
of Sophie and Jean playing ball with the dog. All the cats are deaf.
Steady rain. The music
continues, Charles-Xavier
shouting over the notes, ignoring them: "Beatitude teaches
nothing. To live without
happiness and not wither—
there is an occupation, almost a profession." Take the trees:
we could "contrive to do
without trees," but not leaves,
Charles-Xavier explains from the piano, still playing, "we require
their decorum that is
one of congestion, till
like Shelley we become lewd vegetarians." Apprehensive
about the rain, I ask
Jean to order a closed
carriage for Simone. The doctor frowns—a regular visitor
these days?—and frightens her,
eyeing Sophie's mushrooms;
his diagnosis: toadstools. Scriabin diminishes. Is the dog
lost? Jean rushes outside.
Punishment of the dog:
he is forbidden the strawberry patch. Darker now. One candle
is found for the piano,
and the music resumes
with Debussy, a little sphere of yellow in the sopping dusk.
The river's surface looks—
is it the rain?—like the sea
in shallows: this moment is an instance of the world becoming
a mere convenience,
more or less credible,

and the old questions rise to our lips—but have we spoken a word?—
           before we remember,
             prompted by the weather
probably, or the time of day, that we already know something:
           we are not newborn, then.
           What is it that we know?
The carriage comes at last, but it is an open carriage, merely
           hooded. We crowd under,
            fending off the last drops
with a violet golf umbrella Charles-Xavier has somehow
           managed for us. A slow
           cold drive under the trees,
Simone balancing the suspect mushrooms in her lap. I tell her
           it is not dangerous:
           we cannot die, but are
in this light or lack of it—trees dripping, the sky fraudulent—
           much less individuals
           than we hope or fear to be.
Once home, we shall have a little supper of Sophie's fresh-picked morels.

OSSORIO ASSEMBLES A UNIVERSE

The Creation was an Act of Generosity, not an
Act of Justice.
                                    —*Thomas Aquinas*

You had things enough there to make anyone
        uneasy, I'm not denying that.
The glass eyes alone, or in pairs, reminding
        me of the more unsightly spare parts
cluttering up the slabs in Count Frankenstein's
        ancestral lab . . . The antelope horns,
eland, elk, whatever forked or pronged itself
        into offence, waited in rows for
you to saw them down. Sorted into sizes,
        driftwood littered the beaches of your
intent, along with fur buttons, spurious
        pre-Columbian heads, coq feathers
prepared for another Dietrich revival,
        and it was all to serve something else:

Your Will. Other visitors I know were spooked
        by what Auden calls, in our landscape,
the heterogeneous *dreck* you handled
        so deftly as you steered them around
archipelagos of coral, mulberry
        roots and broken mirrors, readily
avoiding whales' teeth in tarpits of plastic
        which had not yet dried. Who first devised
the nervous gag—that we could shortly expect,
        given the rate you were going now,
to see Someone we knew laid out at length here
        from fontanel to pelvic girdle?

56

So sinister to some your good manners seemed,
    I suppose and, craven, shuddered too.

More accurately, that courtliness of yours,
    the grand seigneurial style no one
of us felt he quite deserved, suggests
    another circle, another sphere—
when callers were shown the Grand Duke's collection
    of coelanaglyphic intaglios,
carnelian seals and Tanagra figurines
    by Councillor von Goethe himself,
who took a curious pleasure, Weimar found,
    in fingering such antiquities.
Appropriate that like Goethe too, you worked
    in an untenanted theater,
commanding your queer creations from the stage
    while we sidled past them on the floor.

For what dismayed us here was no more the smell
    of narwhal tusks macerating than
the sight of seven hundred Cuban tree snails,
    each in its rhinestone socket. What we
quailed at, queasily, was the real heresy
    in these concoctions. God knows you had
given the Fathers every chance, there were still
    Crosses all over the place—chiefly
carved out of treated feces, of course—but not
    even the Church could express for you
the True Cross between what is worth redeeming
    in us and what we are. You would do
that yourself. No wonder if we winced to see
    Mephisto smiling at his wild forge!

DO IT AGAIN: Didactic Stanzas

i   Being! Being! the body rants
When pain is the color of certain events:
     Surely it's better to scream "I suffer"
     Than say "This landscape is ugly."

ii   Comes a time, in the dead of doubt,
When action alone is certainty:
     The heart's still-lifes are still
     Only after a violent death.

iii   Pale in the prospect of my love
Your body lies, a fiction but
     My one chance of saving what
     Time and society erode.

iv   So I return to the gestures of lust
As if it were to innocence:
     Repetition is the only mode
     That nature knows of memory.

A SPEAKING LIKENESS

A lady I knew died not long ago,
    having lately passed
her eighty-seventh year on the planet.
    She had been, they said,
the image of Aunt Emily, and that
    was her surest self,
she explained—a "dead ringer" all her life.

Some years before the end, I remember,
    she defined the phrase
which had to do with horses, fraudulent
    entries in a race,
false names for better odds. That is no sense
    I care to keep, for
Emily's niece was, though equine, genuine

enough despite bewildering contrasts:
    her long bony face
had its abrupt square black brows affording
    the authority
of constraint under cotton-wool hair
    recalled to order
by the cabaline, arched New England nose—

every feature *told,* most the wrinkled mouth
    that told me once—last
probably of all the times the story
    was insisted on—
what afternoons were like in Amherst, days
    when she entertained
the posthumously famous Emily.

"You could say I knew her by ear. She spoke
        to me from the hall
while I sat—age nine—as I was told, not
        looking round to see
my 'peculiar' aunt who would not appear,
        playing my pieces
for her on the sable Chickering grand.

But glimpsed her when I came in, impassive
        as porcelain, hands
folded in her lap, eyes fixed straight ahead.
        She liked Mendelssohn,
would often command, her voice cracked but loud
        enough to carry
over the stylish *presto,* 'try again.'

Not that I blundered so often, the notes
        were nimble in fact,
but for her, trying must have been the word
        for any doing.
Sometimes I think she slid away: I saw
        the window darken
and a long shadow move across the lawn.

I played on, though, in the dim house while she
        obliterated
her life in that secret way she had learned.
        We only learned it
when my mother found them in the attic—
        sewn in neat packets,
all that was left: eighteen hundred poems."

Such was the old lady's story, who became
        soon after, a dead

ringer of the other sort, not having
    Emily's "success
in circuit." The odds were against her. *Wrecked,*
    solitary, here,
the old niece faltered—foundered, like us all

on consternation's carrousel. Poets, farewell
    and goodnight, ladies!
Earth itself must turn to a dead ringer
    in time, speeding round
its unavailing sun. "Circumference
    is my business,"
Emily consoled, an old maid cherishing

the world in her image—all men nieces
    of an absconded
Progenitor (*Burglar, Banker, Father!*)—
    and only concerned
with what she felt could surround. Yet scorned
    the fond foolishness
which every morning "prayed to an Eclipse."

"The mind of the heart must live," she declared,
    more confident with
no doctrine but the bundles left upstairs
    than her dying niece,
like us, could afford to be. There's reason
    we have lost our trust
in the mind as in the heart. *Why* must it live?

The old woman I knew died, the image of
    Emily. Poems
return to the attic or remain there.
    And as the mind rings

its unacknowledged spoil like Gemini,
    the best we can do
is recognize faces, find resemblances.

FOR HEPHAISTOS, WITH REFERENCE TO THE DEATHS IN A DRY YEAR OF COCTEAU, ROETHKE AND MacNEICE

> Whatever I may mean could not be equally
> well conveyed by gestures but can be expressed,
> if at all, in speech (that is why I wish to write
> this poem), and wherever speech is necessary,
> lying and self-deception are both possible.
> —*W. H. Auden*

I come on down the common street, a smear
Of stores like neon sores, where citizens
Whose needs and greeds will never overlap
Are busy buying up their brainless haul
In a Season reasonable merchants fear
Will be far too slack for a rainless fall
(Waiters will give you no water today
Until you tell them to), but painless all
The same for a pining time of the year.

Beside me slides the shadow of my love,
Or the body which cast that shadow once
And darkens my discernment ever since,
And now our shadows, unobserved, remove
Themselves along the pavement, past the place
Where G-men have raided a restaurant
For serving water, past the movie house,
The bar, the bank, and just as we confront
The bookshop you come out: we're face to face.

In a year when the poets are dying
Of madness not murrains, not rot but rage,
And only Great Statesmen live to great age,
When we mourn a forger who died trying
To lock both profiles into the one face

(Only he looked too many ways), and mourn
Our crazy countryman who gave his voice
To the high wind that howled him down, and scorned
All synonyms but violence for grace;

In a year when your Iceland playmate died,
Leaving not much more than a thirties' drawl
And your collaboration, it is all
The more reassuring to find your head
Suddenly bobbing up, surprised, beside
My own in that place, your sane face showing,
By the way it was wrinkled, all that had
Happened outside you, a way of knowing
The Good, more than a way of going bad—

A letter to the future that your life
Had found much crumpled underneath some chair
And hastily smoothed out: I looked, and there
Was no profession in your look back save
A final harmlessness that made it clear
You could not be a bum, despite your air
Of tweedy degeneration. The stare
Exchanged was all that passed between for proof
I knew you, even as my onetime love.

Wondering, I forgot my words and lost
All presence of mind as you labored past.
And yet you taught me, taught us all a way
To speak our minds, and only now, at last
Free of you, my old ventriloquist,
Have I suspected what I have to say
Without hearing you say it for me first.
Like my old love, I have survived you best
By leaving you, and so you're here to stay.

In a thirsty season, then, while we wait
For all the upstate reservoirs to fill,
In a year whose characteristic stamp
Will probably be the admission of "camp"
Into the Unabridged, what better style
Of thanking you for your too-famous state
Of being here, the indescribable
Dasein of this moment—you like a tramp,
My lorn love, the long drouth—than keeping still?

"EVEN THE MOST BEAUTIFUL SUNSET IS BORING IN THREE-QUARTERS OF AN HOUR"

We sat on the deck
of a celebrated decorator
    as the sun declined
and fell to its customary ruin.

"A little applause,"
you drawled, as it finally disappeared,
    "might bring it back up,
seeing how well-rehearsed the performance was."

"Recapitulate—
I dare you—the progress of French landscape,"
    our host exulted,
"from Boudin to Bonnard faster than *that!*"

certain that the sun
had been trained in the greatest ateliers
    to gain such *maîtrise*
where all of Europe's scholars drew—a blank.

"Or else, I should say,"
I said, "the sun had seen far too many
    Japanese movies
for its own good as a cameraman."

You laughed at us both
and reported how as a girl in Holland
    you watched the sun fade
from the terrace, over the flat red fields,

and then ran upstairs
to see it vanish all over again.
    "Which was, I suppose,"
you ended, "what is known as a Dutch treat."

    Our host reminded
us about Goethe's put-down of sunsets . . .
    Besides, it was dark.
Soon we went indoors and turned on some lights.

OYSTERING

Secret they are, sealed, annealed, and brainless
And solitary as Dickens said, but
They have something to say: that there is more
Than one way to yield. The first—and the hardest,
The most nearly hindered—is when you pull
Them off the rocks, a stinking, sawing sedge
Sucking them back under the black mud, full
Of hermit crabs and their borrowed snailshells,
Minnows scattering like superstitions,
The surf dragging, and every power
Life permits them holding out, holding on
For dear life. Sometimes the stones give way first,
Before *they* will, but still we gather them,
Even if our hands are bloody as meat,
For a lunch Queen Victoria preferred:
"A barrel of Wellfleet oysters, points down"
Could last across the ocean, all the way
To Windsor, wakening a widow's taste.
We ate them this afternoon, out of their
Armor that was formidably grooved, though
It proved our own reversal wiser still:
Keep the bones and stones inside, or never
Leave the sea. "He was a brave man," Swift said,
"Who first eat one." Even now, precedent
Of centuries is not always enough.
Driving the knife into muscles that mould
The valves so close to being impartial,
Surrender, when it comes—and it must come:

Lavish after that first grudging release
Back there in the sea, the giving over
Of despair, this time—makes me speculate.
Like Oscar and oysters, I feel "always
Slightly immortal when in the sea": what
Happens now we are out? Is the risk worth
While for a potential pearl? No, what we're
Really after is the moment of release,
The turn and tear of the blade that tightens,
Tortures, ultimately tells. When you spread
The shells, something always sticks to the wrong
One, and a few drops of liquor dribble
Into the sand. Scrape it off: in the full
Half, as well as a Fautrier, a Zen
Garden, and the smell of herring brine that
Ferenczi said we remember from the womb,
Lunch is served, in shiny stoneware sockets,
Blue milk in the sea's filthiest cup. More
Easily an emblem for the inner man
Than dinner, sundered, for the stomach. We
Take them queasily, wonder as we gulp
When it is—then, now, tomorrow—they're dead.

THE AUTHOR OF 'CHRISTINE'

For Sanford Friedman

Often waking
before the sun decreed the kind of day
                    this one would be
            or by its absence left
            the verdict up to him,
he gazed in doubt
at the blank slate and wondered, blue or gray,
                    what *he* might leave
            scribbled against the time
            the darkness came for good;
that was his text.
The trouble was, he realized, to choose.
                    He roused the rooms,
            walking around the house
            that had to share the day
with his despair,
raising each blind as if it were the dead,
                    the morning light
            a record of his progress
            in sudden shafts of dust.
The trouble was
in trying so: imagining Christine
                    to be this way
            or that. Reality
            had to be happened on,
one had to *find,*
not create it. There is always life itself
                    beyond the prose
            that declares it to us,
            life being an absolute

70

we aspire to,
bliss, but surely cannot reach. Today
he would write more,
creating in Christine
his hopes of what was real,
knowing 'the real'
by what becomes of it and of ourselves.
Dust was his proof:
the life we know we live
is simply not enough:
the work dissolves,
leaches into the medium and is lost
there like water;
the words sink into sand,
dust dances in the sun.
Christine was chaos,
parcels of his own childhood where the past
appeared to be
no more than behavior,
merely authority.
Take the big scene
when Giorgio, leaving the attic, hobbles down
and asks Christine
about the box, she pales
and follows him back—why?
"The novelist
seldom penetrates character, the mystery
remains intact."
Thank you Thomas Hardy,
sighing over the mess
you made for her
yet asking "Where was Tess's guardian angel *then?*"
He much preferred
Hardy the poet now,

that doubting Thomas who
when Swinburne died
declared him "the sweet rival of the waves
                    and once their peer
          in sad improvisations."
          That was character.
To make Christine
out of what was not his choice, participate
                    in what would change
          her, like the waves, and him . . .
          Shoving his desk outside
into the sun,
he decided *Christine* could not be written from
                    his waking hopes:
          by will to set himself
          or the reader apart
from what the world
might be without the waves, bereft of wet
                    and wilderness.
          No, he would have to let
          the weeds of wavering
flourish, rehearse
to both of them, the reader and himself,
                    not ways that help
          us on but that will help
          acknowledge our defeat
in getting on—
that would be *Christine,* his novel, and
                    Christine be him.

AN OLD DANCER

Because there is only one of you in all of time
. . . the world will not have it . . .
    — *Martha Graham*

Your props had always been important:
Preposterous poniards, rings and thorns,
Things without a name you fell upon
Or through. Now they are your props indeed.
Take that iron prong you dangle from,
Strung up, slung like a sick animal
Who used to rise as straight as any tree
Without such corporal irony.

Propped then, you make no bones, or only
Bones, of husbanding your strength. For strength
Was your husband, and you're widowed now.
The face that was a mask of wonder
Wizens into the meaninglessness
Of some Osaka marionette,
And there is properly little more
That you can do for us than think.

What thoughts are yours, or were yours when
Half-visionary and half-voyeur
You tore the veils from Remembered Women,
Rarely lovely, except as the space
That took them into its hugest mouth
Makes any movement lovely: at first
It was enough for you to be them,
Violent, often vague as they come,

73

Until the years and the work of years
Led you beyond being into more
Than self supplied: now you must review
What you have been and let the others
Do. What you were a whole theater
Has become. What have you lost by that
Exchange, save as the tree loses by
Giving up its leaves and standing bare?

O Dancer, you have lost everything,
Shuddering on your iron gallows-tree.
Bane, bone and violence, you answer
Yeats in kind, unkindest witch of all:
"We know the dancer from the dance" by age,
By growing old. The dance goes on,
The dancers go, and you hang here
Like stale meat on your dead steel branch.

THE ENCOUNTER

The landscape—at least what you can see of it,
        for these are contours that afford
    no rest, no recompense after a long
stare, the very air drinks down the scenery,
        all but a yellow scum the sun
        deposits round the bottom of the glass—
the landscape is the color *lion*, the low
        hills like a ring of lions then.
    The light leaves nothing upright in your mind.
There are no birds. Noon, it must be always noon,
        the way your shadow dribbles out
    into the sand: if the sun were modest
would it be the sun? And you have been walking
        toward those same mountains forever.
    Have they changed at all? Is there even one
tree to tell by? Whatever lies between you
        and the edge of existence
    makes no sign. There is the desert and there
is the sky: daylight is the way things behave.
        The ridges of pale sand, in rows,
    parody oceans, and just as you climb
over the next one you see something shipwrecked—
        ribs of a boat that has been starved
    to death? As you approach, the boat dissolves
into a Being like a giant insect,
        spider? spider-crab? What is it, sprawled
    on a stretch of Nowhere that somehow leads
your mind back to the other Thebes? Whatever
        waits there, motionless, is ready
    to take you on, turning into itself
as you come, until you learn. Surely it is
        Egyptian enough to find her

here (for you see *her* now), isolated
as much as you are, but all the same at home.
        She has the posture of lions,
    and closing in on her you recognize
what first had fooled you into superstition:
            the spidery legs are simply
        articulated rods attached to what
appears a diving board, where the insolent
            fringe of red-beaded tassels hangs
        swaying even in this exhausted air,
eight feet up, or twelve—in the heat, everything
            looks bigger, distances deceive,
        your memory stops meaning anything.
All that matters is the ring of ragged hills
            behind you and ahead of you
        which suddenly funnel down to her. Her,
up there on a plush platform whose silver legs
            thrust like crooked telescopes
    into the sand. You seem to hesitate
a second, then swing the sweaty leather cloak
            down from one shoulder and drop it
        hissing as it subsides behind your heels.
Now you go straight up to her, not hurrying
            but not holding back either,
        until you stand just where the platform casts
a tiny oblong of shadow. Nothing moves.
            She hunches above you, arms flat,
        and you can see her nails over the rim:
they are silver too. You grab the rope ladder—
            what else is there to do? You look
        up once, look back, and then begin to climb . . .
The ladder shifts with your weight, all the ropes creak
            helplessly, rung by rung, until
        your head appears above the silly fringe.

"It's a little girl, that's all she is, a child!"
        startled, as your eyes come level
    with her hard breasts, you think, "This won't take long."
But then, slinging one leg up, you discover
        what you had to see to believe:
    the need in her expectant loins, betrayed
by a tremor that seems to dim the bright hair
        sprouting like wheat across her hips
    (all your ideas about children change).
The girl lies still, still peering without alarm
        over her intricate shoulder
    as your other leg clears the tassels now:
you are beside her. As if her body yawned,
        she celebrates your being here
    by rolling over lazily, lightly,
looming above you like a lioness then
        and lays one talon on your chest.
    You let your eyes travel the distance up
her arms to where her face hangs toward you, clustered
        just above the beginner's breasts
    too firm to be pendulous; you fondle them
a while and trail one hand along her belly
        to where the long thighs arch over
    your own. She is an animal on you,
a smooth beast grateful for the rough appetite
        within her—how the gratitude
    rages in her exultant flesh, even
to yours! Naked and lovely, the muscles slide,
        then tighten till she is standing,
    warm feet against your rib cage, and you gaze
up the gold columns, past the foreshortened fleece,
        the minor breasts, to where she smiles.
    You loved her on all fours, you love
her standing more, the way we love the naked

always: it is ourselves we love.
The memory awakens, you recall
what you can do with yourself. And first of all
you can perpetuate yourself:
your hands slide up her parted thighs as if
on pulleys, her knees perform, and suddenly
she is down, and only one thing
stands now, ready as your senseless senses
let you know that she is ready too. Impaled
abruptly on the prong of flesh
she writhes, yet you do not move, it is her
moving that sends the answer deeper in, still
deeper, till with a scream she knows
you know. But had there been a question? When
was it put—when the pale animal topped you,
or when the woman made you praise
her where she stood, or when between your legs
you pinned her like a thrush upon a thorn: man.
Nothing is hard now, all the rage
that called you into question dies down to
something poor, exhausted, and a little cold.
The animal sighs, and her breath
goes sour. Forgetting where you are, you push
away the fishy thing, and with a sucking sound
her suddenly gray belly rolls off,
rolls over again, until her legs catch
in the ladder. Down spills her body, knees hooked,
hair reaching almost to the sand,
and if you will descend at all you must
employ the ladder of her limbs. You do it,
retching every time your hand
skids on the oily hide . . . You touch the ground
ahead of your shadow, stand a moment more
there where she dangles to a halt.

The sun has not shifted, yet from somewhere
in an altered sky you hear a terrible
        chord, a crash as of thunder but
     shrieking too, as you reach out and shove her,
just once, to see what she will do. Not a thing.
        "Little girls!" you think, dismissing
     what had almost been a doubt, "the next time
let it be a woman ripe enough to last."
        You lean over, pick up your cloak
     and for all the folly of the sun, spread
it on your shoulders, starting up the long grade
        easily to where you must go.
     The sand gives like a skin under your soles.
Do you look back once? Yes, once, to discover
        that the insect you had supposed
     you saw is there again: down in the pit
out of which you are toiling now, an ant lion
        attends. You are almost too far,
     in another minute or so, to tell
what hangs down from it. Again there is no more
        than a bug behind you, nothing
     more. The ring of dirty hills reappears
at closer range. A bird materializes
        out of nowhere, somehow, singing
     and you know you must be nearer to Thebes
than all the leagues of empty sand can show. Like
        a hero, you are on your way.

Distinguished contemporary poetry in cloth and paperback editions

ALAN ANSEN: *Disorderly Houses* (1961)

JOHN ASHBERY: *The Tennis Court Oath* (1962)

ROBERT BAGG: *Madonna of the Cello* (1961)

ROBERT BLY: *Silence in the Snowy Fields* (1962)

TURNER CASSITY: *Watchboy, What of the Night?* (1966)

TRAM COMBS: *saint thomas. poems.* (1965)

DONALD DAVIE: *Events and Wisdoms* (1965); *New and Selected Poems* (1961)

JAMES DICKEY: *Buckdancer's Choice* (1965) [National Book Award in Poetry, 1966]; *Drowning With Others* (1962); *Helmets* (1964)

DAVID FERRY: *On the Way to the Island* (1960)

ROBERT FRANCIS: *The Orb Weaver* (1960)

JOHN HAINES: *Winter News* (1966)

RICHARD HOWARD: *The Damages* (1967); *Quantities* (1962)

BARBARA HOWES: *Light and Dark* (1959)

DAVID IGNATOW: *Figures of the Human* (1964); *Say Pardon* (1961)

DONALD JUSTICE: *Night Light* (1967); *The Summer Anniversaries* (1960) [A Lamont Poetry Selection]

CHESTER KALLMAN: *Absent and Present* (1963)

LOU LIPSITZ: *Cold Water* (1967)

JOSEPHINE MILES: *Kinds of Affection* (1967)

VASSAR MILLER: *My Bones Being Wiser* (1963); *Wage War on Silence* (1960)

W. R. MOSES: *Identities* (1965)

DONALD PETERSEN: *The Spectral Boy* (1964)

HYAM PLUTZIK: *Apples from Shinar* (1959)

VERN RUTSALA: *The Window* (1964)

HARVEY SHAPIRO: *Battle Report* (1966)

JON SILKIN: *Poems New and Selected* (1966)

LOUIS SIMPSON: *At the End of the Open Road* (1963) [Pulitzer Prize in Poetry, 1964]; *A Dream of Governors* (1959)

JAMES WRIGHT: *The Branch Will Not Break* (1963); *Saint Judas* (1959)